INSTRUCTIONAL MEDIA CENTER
William D. McIntyre Library
University of Wisconsin
Eau Claire, Wisconsin

DISCARDED

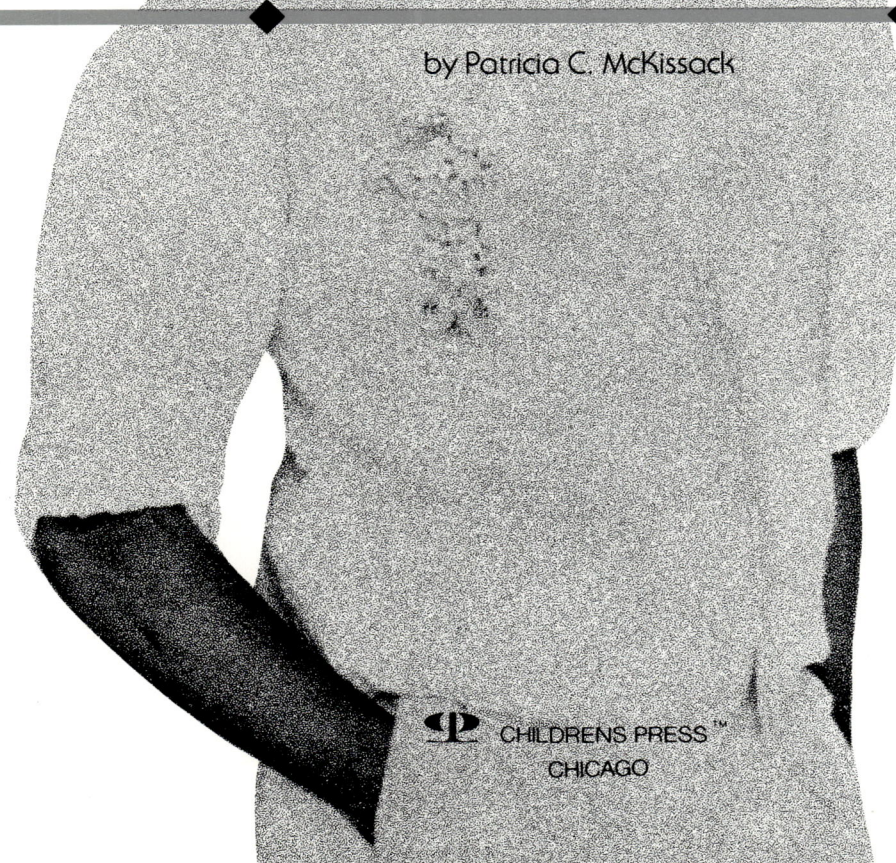

MICHAEL JACKSON, SUPERSTAR!

by Patricia C. McKissack

CHILDRENS PRESS™
CHICAGO

DEDICATION
To my nephew, Willie Davis, Jr.

MICHAEL JACKSON:
"The boy is bad, bad, bad, and I still don't think he's as good as he's gonna be. You know what I mean?"

From THE MICHAEL JACKSON STORY, by Nelson George

Cover and interior design by Karen A. Yops

PHOTO CREDITS
© Charles Dillard—11, 13, 21
© R. Flanagan/Image Finders—9
© Debbie Leavitt, Pix Int'l/Hillstrom Stock Photo—10 (left)
Movie Star News—Back cover, 4, 81
© Paul Natkin/Photo Reserve—58 (top)
Pepsi-Cola, U.S.A.—87
Personality Photos, Inc.—6, 15, 16, 18, 27, 28, 31, 35, 41, 45, 56, 58 (bottom), 77, 84, 85
Retna, LTD.—39
  © Fin Costello—23, 62 (2 photos),
  © Chris Walter—36 (left), 69,
  © Robin Kaplan—36 (right),
  © Simon Fowler—43,
  © Kevin Mazur—74,
  © E.A. Retna, LTD.—70
© Ebet Roberts—Front cover, 7, 10 (right), 37 (2 photos), 46, 59, 61 (left), 67, 75, 88 (top)
UPI—3, 51, 53, 61 (right), 76
Wide World—20, 25, 33, 49, 55, 57, 60, 63, 65, 73, 78, 79, 82, 83, 88 (bottom), 89, 90, 91

Library of Congress Cataloging in Publication Data

McKissack, Pat, 1944-
  Michael Jackon, Superstar

  Includes index.
  Summary: A biography of the wildly popular rock
    musician who is "painfully shy" in his private life.
    1. Jackson, Michael, 1958- —Juvenile literature.
2. Rock musicians—United States—Biography—Juvenile
literature. [1. Jackson, Michael, 1958-
2. Musicians] I. Title. II. Series.
ML3930.J25M3 1984 784.5'4'00924 [B] [92] 84-12070
ISBN 0-516-04380-3

Copyright © 1984 by Regensteiner Publishing Enterprises, Inc.
All rights reserved. Published simultaneously in Canada.
Printed in the United States of America.
1 2 3 4 5 6 7 8 9 10 R 93 92 91 90 89 88 87 86 85 84

Table of Contents

Preface	6	
Introduction	8	
Chapter 1	THE CHITLIN' CIRCUIT	12
Chapter 2	THE BUBBLE-GUM SOUND	22
Chapter 3	THOSE JACKSON BROTHERS	30
Chapter 4	THE JACKSON/MOTOWN SPLIT	38
Chapter 5	THE SECOND GENERATION	44
Chapter 6	EASING ON DOWN THE ROAD	48
Chapter 7	MICHAEL AND FRIENDS	54
Chapter 8	TWO GENIUSES	64
Chapter 9	THE MAGIC OF *THRILLER*	68
Chapter 10	THE LOOK	74
Chapter 11	OFF-STAGE WITH MICHAEL	80
Epilogue	86	
Time Line	92	
Fact Sheet	94	
Index	95	

Preface

Michael Jackson is an extraordinary performer who has had years of stage experience. When most eleven-year-olds were riding bicycles and going to summer camp, Michael Jackson was already working on stage with his brothers. They were known the world over as the Jackson Five. Years later, that eleven-year-old revolutionized the way we listen to music. Today he is considered to be America's superstar. Each of his performances is an electrifying display of talent and energy.

Without a doubt, Michael is a superstar, loved by millions. Yet what do we know about him? He's a Virgo; he is very ticklish; he loves children and animals; he won eight Grammy Awards for his album *Thriller*; and he is painfully shy, except when he's onstage. Then he is said to "sing like an angel and dance like a demon." That sums up about everything that has been written about him.

Michael Jackson is one of the most popular performers in the world; yet his fans know very little about him. He does not grant many interviews and he refuses to answer personal questions, especially about his wealth. He chooses to keep his

The Jackson brothers perform before an enthusiastic audience at the Nassau Coliseum in Queens, New York. The 1979 performance thrilled spectators and successfully pushed the Jackson career into the 80s.

private life separate from his public life—and that is his right.

Maybe one day Michael will tell his own story. Then many questions will be answered, or perhaps more will be raised. In the meantime his fans want to know about him—now! This is the story of the ''public'' Michael with a few of the glimpses of his inner world he has chosen to share.

In compiling the information in this book I used newspapers, magazines, and previously written books. I wish to thank Clare Coffey for her help in researching this book, the staff at the University City Library, and my husband, Fredrick McKissack, without whose help this book could not have been completed.

Patricia C. McKissack
St. Louis, Missouri
April, 1984

Introduction
THE JACKSONS OF JACKSON STREET

Joseph and Katherine Jackson were married in 1949. He was twenty-one and she was eighteen. They settled in Gary, Indiana, and by 1969 were the proud parents of nine children. Maureen, the firstborn, was followed by Jackie, Tito, Jermaine, LaToya, Marlon, Michael, Randy, and Janet—otherwise known as the Jacksons of Jackson Street.

During the early years of their marriage, Joe Jackson had wanted to be an entertainer and, for a while, had played guitar and sung with a group called the Falcons. The group's performances were limited to local clubs and colleges. Katherine Jackson, by some reports, was a singer of semiprofessional status, too.

But the Jackson children came fast. And, though a part of Joe Jackson was a dreamer, he also had a practical side. He faced reality. There were babies to feed, shoes to buy, and bills to pay. That didn't leave much time for pursuing a musical career, and Joe wasn't the kind of man to duck his responsibilities. So, he accepted the challenges of parenting and decided to become the best father he could. Joe Jackson was the undisputed head of his

A one-way sign in front of the Jackson home in Gary, Indiana, points north. The Jacksons traveled north and east to sign with Detroit-based Motown records in 1968.

Mr. Joseph Jackson is interviewed by a reporter from "Entertainment Tonight."

Katherine Jackson, mother of the nine Jackson children, poses for a camera at a recent California luncheon.

household—the provider and protector.

Katherine Jackson also slipped comfortably into her role as full-time homemaker. She made 825 Jackson Street a warm and wonderful home for her large and active family, while Joe worked as a crane operator at one of Gary's steel companies. Some sources say that Katherine also worked—at Sear's department store—but if she did, it must have been only part-time or seasonal.

The 1960s were difficult years—a time when drug use was rising and parental authority was declining. Gary, often called "Sin City," was a small, tough town not too far from Chicago. Unemployment was high, the success rate among blacks was low, and self-esteem was even lower.

Since there wasn't a lot to do or to look forward to doing, many of the neighborhood kids just "hung out." But not the Jackson kids. Papa Joe knew the ever-present dangers and temptations of a large urban center. He didn't want any of his children suffering the consequences of unchecked "running in the streets."

Both Jackson parents set high standards for their children. Back in Kentucky, where Joe had grown up, his father, a teacher, had taught him that hard work and discipline were the keys to success. Joe believed in his father's philosophy and used it to keep his children on a straight and narrow path.

Papa Joe believed that a sure way of keeping his children off the streets and out of trouble was to channel their interests and energies into wholesome and constructive activities, such as singing and sports. Katherine agreed. She also knew the importance of persistence in trying to achieve a life goal.

At a very young age, Katherine Jackson had been stricken with polio—a crippling disease. But, she had walked. Faith, she believes, has always been the deciding factor in her life. Katherine's strong religious beliefs—she is a Jehovah's Witness—became the foundation of the family's moral development.

Take hard work and constant discipline, reinforce these with faith, and bind them with love. The result is success. It worked for one family—the Jacksons of Jackson Street. And the formula is still working for their seventh child—Michael Joseph Jackson, superstar!

Mayor Richard Hatcher walks behind young Michael (left) on their way to a 1968 fund-raising event at West Side High School in Gary. Some say it was at this event that the Jackson Five were first discovered.

Chapter 1
THE CHITLIN' CIRCUIT

Michael Joseph Jackson was born in Gary, Indiana, on August 29, 1958, the seventh child in a large and growing family. He launched his singing career at school, surprising his kindergarten teacher with a soulful version of "Climb Every Mountain." His brothers—Jackie, Tito, and Jermaine—had been performing as a trio for several years before that.

While Michael was still in elementary school, he joined his older brothers' act. They performed on stages throughout America as the Jackson Five—the best of the bubble gum groups. Their first hit singles, "I Want You Back" (1969) and "ABC" (1970), skyrocketed them to international fame. At the time of their first success, Michael, the lead singer, was only eleven years old, but he and his brothers were already show-business veterans with five years of experience under their belts.

In the early 1970s, when the group had become well known, they were asked how they had gotten started. The Jacksons gave full credit to their parents. Michael has been quoted as saying, "Nobody discovered the Jackson Five except our mother and father."

In hope of gaining stage experience and more publicity, the Jacksons performed at every talent show sponsored in Gary. Even at the age of nine, Michael (second from right) charmed audiences with his attractive style.

According to numerous accounts, the Jackson Five got their start in the mid-1960s. By then, Joe Jackson had given up his dream of becoming a singing star, but he kept his guitar around as a remembrance. He had warned his children that his guitar was not a toy. It was an instrument that was to be played but never played with. No one was to touch Papa Joe's guitar.

Meanwhile, Katherine Jackson had been encouraging her children to sing and dance. "It came naturally," she said, explaining her children's talents. As a concerned mother, Katherine saw singing and dancing as a way to keep her children happy and occupied—especially after the television set broke down and there was no extra money to get it repaired right away.

Without Joe's knowing it, Tito, his second son (and the son said to be most like his father), was learning how to play the guitar—really play it—and he often added a little zip to the family singing by accompanying the group on Papa Joe's guitar. Even then, as a toddler, Michael beat out the song rhythms on tabletops.

One day Papa Joe caught Tito playing his prize guitar. Michael remembers the incident well. "My father caught Tito with the guitar and he got so mad...he whipped him, let him have it. Then he said to Tito, 'Let me see what you can do.' And he meant it. Well, Tito picked up the guitar and started playing. My father was shocked 'cause he saw some special talent there. He was really surprised. He was so happy his son could do this."

Joe's anger turned to surprise, then delight. He listened to his sons' singing. He watched them dance. They were good—not because they were his sons—there was real talent working. Sure, he saw that it was raw talent—they would need a lot of work—but they were good! Better than good. And, they seemed to love it.

Right away, Jackie, Tito, and Jermaine, the three oldest sons, formed the first Jackson group. Jermaine was the first lead singer. At first the trio performed locally and in minor talent shows. Marlon joined the group when he was six years old and Michael became a member at the age of five. When the group decided to make Michael the lead singer, the sound and the style of the group was set for the next decade. A neighbor dubbed them the Jackson Five (sometimes written Jackson-5, Jackson 5ive, or just J-5). The name was adopted, and an American legend was born.

With Michael singing lead, the group walked away with first-place talent show

The combined talent of Jackie (top right), Tito, Jermaine (bottom left), Marlon, and Michael appealed to young fans.

Jackson 5

Among the artists who most influenced Michael is the dynamic Ray Charles.

honors and trophies in Illinois and Indiana, often winning against older and more experienced competitors. Pint-sized Michael Jackson charmed audiences with his showmanship, which closely resembled the style of his favorite performer at that time, James Brown.

Brown, known in the sixties as the "King of Soul Music," had a great influence on the Jackson Five—especially on young Michael, who studied the superstar's flamboyant style and mastered his complicated movements jerk for jerk, twist for twist.

Other artists who impressed young Michael at the time were Sam Cooke, the Temptations, Lou Rawls, the Miracles, and Sam and Dave. In the early days, the Jacksons included these stars' songs in their programs. "Mickey's Monkey" by the Miracles and an all-time favorite of the mid-sixties, "Hold On, I'm Coming" by Sam and Dave, were sure crowd pleasers —especially when sung by a little boy who had as much pizzazz as the original performers. It was more than just cute. The Jackson brothers were bonafide entertainers with talent rarely so polished in youngsters their ages.

The Jacksons' style was typical of rock groups during that period—a driving beat and repetitive lyrics. Mostly they imitated the sounds of other popular groups, but with amazing originality of style. Their uniqueness lay in their youth and in the fact that they were brothers. Adults marveled that such sounds could come from children.

No audience, regardless of age, could sit still and listen to the Jackson Five. In a recent article in *Time* magazine (March 19, 1984), Rufus Morgan recalled a performance the J-5 gave when they were still amateurs in Gary. Morgan had arranged for the group to perform at a fund raiser. "Those boys were so fascinating to watch" he says, "that everybody just gathered around the stage. We didn't dance. We watched and threw money."

For a while Papa Joe still worked at the factory, and the boys were still in school. During the evenings and on weekends and vacations, they practiced and practiced—long hard hours of practice. In the winter when there really wasn't much to do, practicing wasn't so bad. But in the summer when the sounds of their friends playing ball in the park behind their house filtered through the window, it was awful. That made no difference to Papa Joe. Practice came first. No matter what, the group practiced. Joe was serious about his boys' careers. And after a while, his sons became serious, too.

Unfortunately, the neighbors didn't always share the Jacksons' enthusiasm for music or their dedication. It was not uncommon for a rock to come sailing through the Jacksons' window, followed by harsh insults and a series of negative comments. "Why are you trying so hard? Nothing will ever come of it."

Joe Jackson remembers those times well. "When I saw that they [the boys] liked it, I kept them at it. I helped them when it got hard for them and when they felt disgusted as kids sometimes do...."

After a while the Jacksons began to get engagements that paid. Joe quit his job to become their manager. Katherine was concerned, but she did not question her husband's motives. She joined in and helped by sewing the stage outfits on her Singer sewing machine, and she always offered moral support.

Papa Joe remembers, "I didn't want to deny them the opportunity to have this profession, and I didn't want them to be managed by a stranger who might let them run wild. So, I quit my job at the steel mill and gave my time to the show business part of it."

Since that time the question has been raised as to whether Joe and Katherine pushed their children or tried to live out their fantasies through their children.

Early in his career Michael mimicked the style and moves of James Brown.

Tito, the second oldest Jackson Fiver, responded during a 1972 interview, "Our parents did push us, but not against our will. We loved music, it was a thrill to be making music at that age that sounded good and that adults seemed to like...."

Papa Joe told *Time* magazine reporter Denise Worrell, in a 1984 interview, "They [his sons] got a little upset about the whole thing in the beginning because the other kids were out there having a good time.... Then I saw that after they became better they enjoyed it more...."

Joe put his philosophy of hard work and discipline into practice over and over again. The rehearsals he insisted on were rigorous, but worthwhile. He has said, "If I had it to do over again, I'd do it the same way.... I don't want to brag, but looking at the kids I think I've done a good job. It was hard, but it sure has paid off."

Before long the Jacksons were getting recognition from show-business professionals who caught their act. Once the Jackson Five was the opening act for the Jerry Butler show. Papa Joe's boys put on such a fantastic show that Freddie Perren, then a performer with Jerry Butler (and later a well-known songwriter), was so impressed with the youngsters' professionalism that he never forgot them. Gladys Knight also saw the Jackson Five perform and was quite taken with the group's style and audience appeal. These would be two important contacts. It was this kind of exposure that Joe Jackson worked at getting for his sons.

Many people aren't aware that the Jackson Five's first records were not recorded with Motown. Their first single, "I'm a Big Boy Now," was recorded on the Steeltown label, a recording company located in Gary. Michael sang the lead. It wasn't a bad cut, and although it didn't get promoted outside the Midwest, it was a local hit of sorts.

The J-5 cut another record, "Jam Session," which was at best mediocre. But it is interesting to note that Papa Joe played the electric guitar on this disc. It is his only recorded performance. Today these two records are considered collectors' items.

The Jackson Five began to build their reputation by winning talent shows. Papa Joe allowed the boys to entertain anywhere they could get exposure and onstage experience. Against Katherine's wishes, Joe allowed the boys to perform in local nightclubs. Michael recalls the time from a child's point of view: "When we would sing, people would throw this money on the floor. Tons of dollars, tens, twenties, lots of change. I remember my pockets being so full of money that I couldn't keep my pants up. I'd wear a real tight belt. And I'd buy candy like crazy." Some nights the group would pick up as much as $300.

From 1967 to 1968 the Jackson Five worked hard to polish their act. Their goal was to perform at the Apollo Theater in Harlem, New York. Every Wednesday night was amateur night at the Apollo. Since they had won all the top talent shows in Indiana and Illinois, Papa Joe felt that his boys were ready for the challenge. The Apollo was a must for black acts trying to get discovered. Some of the giants in the industry had performed on the Apollo stage—Stevie Wonder for one.

The Jackson Five got their invitation during the summer of 1968. "I remember the night of the show," says Joe Jackson. "The kids were so nervous.... They wanted the crowd to like them."

The kids needn't have worried. The loud and often unruly crowd gave the J-5 a standing ovation—something that didn't happen often. Apollo crowds were known to be a hard audience to please.

From that point on, the J-5 were invited to perform everywhere—from local political rallies to nightclubs in Chicago. They became a star attraction on the "Chitlin' Circuit"—a group of theaters and nightclubs around the country that regularly booked black entertainers.

Papa Joe would load the boys and the baggage into their VW van. On weekends and during summer vacation they went from stage to stage, city to city—Philadelphia, New York, Washington, D.C., Kansas City, Chicago. It was long, hard work, but it was fun, too.

Papa Joe used the long road hours to critique his sons' performance. They also played cards and talked about the future and the Jackson Five's place in it. Then they would all try to get some sleep.

Often Michael and his brothers got home from a tour just in time to wash, eat a quick breakfast, and dash off to school. In a 1972 *Scholastic Review* interview,

Jermaine laughed about how hard it was to stay awake during class. But he was quick to add that school and good grades were no laughing matter to his parents.

Joe and Katherine Jackson stressed good grades and good study habits. All the children had household chores to do, and telephone calls were limited to five minutes. Punishments were given for misbehavior—usually no allowance.

During those road trips, Michael learned a lot about entertaining from some of the best in the industry—like the smooth and stylish Temptations. Michael practiced their moves and imitated the way they worked the microphone. Even then, Michael was shy and chose to look at his show-business favorites from a distance rather than introduce himself.

The Chitlin' Circuit was not glamorous. It was work. Joe saw it as valuable training and a necessary stepping stone to the group's success. Katherine was getting her wish, too; she was keeping her family together and happy. The boys? Well, their stars were just beginning to rise.

The Temptations were at the top of the Jackson list of show-business favorites.

Chapter 2

THE BUBBLE-GUM SOUND

There are many stories about how the Jackson Five came to Motown. One of the most popular versions is that Diana Ross discovered them while she was entertaining in Gary. Other sources credit Gladys Knight, and still others say that Bobby Taylor, another Motown recording artist, was responsible for getting the Jackson Five a hearing before Berry Gordy. In truth all of them played a part in the Jackson Five's story.

The year of the Jackson Five was 1968. Richard Hatcher, Gary's first black mayor, was holding a fund raiser. Because he and Papa Joe were friends, Hatcher arranged for the group to open for Diana Ross and the Supremes, who were at that time Motown super-superstars. Diana Ross listened to the Jackson Five and "fell in love with their sound." Young Michael reminded the flashy lead singer, who had grown up in a large family in a housing project in Detroit, of herself as a child—talented and filled with energy and wide-eyed enthusiasm. She couldn't help but be impressed by Michael and his brothers.

"I looked at this little kid whirling around up there and I thought I was look-

The Jackson Five proudly pose for a publicity shot. Standing are Jackie, the oldest (left), and Jermaine. Sitting are Tito (right), Michael, and Marlon. Randy, the youngest (not pictured), was not yet part of the group.

ing at myself. I couldn't believe it. I thought the group was terrific, so I asked them if they'd like to meet the head of my record company, Berry Gordy, Jr. I saw so much of myself as a child in Michael. He was performing all the time. That's the way I was. He could be my son." Diana Ross was true to her word. She went to Berry Gordy, president of the Motown recording studio, and convinced him to let the group audition for him.

Papa Joe says that there were intermediate steps that are often overlooked. The Jackson Five were not totally unknown to Motown when Diana Ross approached Gordy on their behalf. Joe had sent Motown a tape several years earlier. Also other Motown artists, such as Gladys Knight, had been putting in a good word for the group. Joe Jackson says that Diana Ross was responsible for helping the group get through the door, but the Jackson Five were already on the threshold of making it big. Their father was convinced then, and believes to this day, that his sons were ready—it was just a matter of its being their time.

The group performed at the Gordy mansion in Detroit and was a success. They knew it. They were happy with their performance and felt sure they would be offered a contract. But Gordy was in the process of relocating his company in Los Angeles and the contract didn't come right away. Jackie, the oldest, recalled how nervous they all were waiting for that call to come. All other telephone calls were restricted to one minute. Finally the call came. The Jackson Five were going to Los Angeles. They were officially a Motown act.

Motown. What did that mean? The name Motown stands for "Motor Town," a name for Detroit, Michigan, the home of the automotive industry. Berry Gordy, Jr., the founder of Motown records, had worked in one of Detroit's automobile factories. But he knew that was not his life's work. He had tried boxing. He had written a few songs. But what he really wanted was a recording company of his own. So, in the late 1950s, Berry Gordy started Motown with $800 and a lot of heart. By the late 1960s Motown was one of the largest recording companies in the world—and a multimillion-dollar concern.

Gordy handpicked young black talent that might otherwise have gone unnoticed and shaped and molded them into superstars. The world has Berry Gordy to thank for recording the sounds of Smokey Robinson and the Miracles, Marvin Gaye, the Temptations, Stevie Wonder, Martha and the Vandellas, and Diana Ross and the Supremes. In 1968 the Jackson Five became the newest addition to the Motown family.

Gordy had also moved his personal residence to Los Angeles. When the call came that the Jackson family was to move to Los Angeles, Michael was assigned to live with Diana Ross. His parents and brothers stayed with Gordy.

Michael's stay with Diana Ross marked the beginning of their long and lasting friendship. He recalled later, "It was like heaven. We went to Disneyland," he continued. "We had fun every day...." Diana became Michael's teacher, his mentor, his "other mother," and most important, his friend. Michael has often said he can tell Diana Ross his "deepest, darkest secrets."

Although the contract was signed in 1968, the Jackson Five's first record was not released until 1969, and they didn't make their first public appearances until the fall of 1969 and early winter of 1970. Why? That was the Berry Gordy/Motown way. Berry Gordy was an image maker. Under his direction, all Motown artists were groomed before being introduced to the public. If they were destined to be stars, then they had to be ready. So, he coached his artists in the social graces—

Berry Gordy (right), president and founder of Motown records, joins veteran entertainer Smokey Robinson on a Los Angeles stage.

how to walk, how to sit, how to speak, how to eat. Then he gave them a "look" that fit the public image he wanted them to have.

It is believed that during the period between signing the contract and the release of their first record, the Jackson Five were being trained. Michael was Diana's responsibility. Other sources say Gordy was waiting for the right song to give the group a super sendoff. Whatever the reason for waiting, it was worth it.

The song they recorded, "I Want You

Back," was written by Freddie Perren—the young songwriter who had seen the Jacksons years earlier. He was now with Motown as a songwriter and was part of a group called the Corporation, which consisted of Berry Gordy, Jr., Deke Richards, Fonce Mizell, and Freddie Perren. Originally the song had been written for Gladys Knight, but Berry sent Freddie back to the sound studio with instructions to rewrite the song to fit the Jackson Five.

The results were phenomenal. The lyrics were fun, and the beat meant dance... dance... dance to teenagers.

Following the success of "I Want You Back," the Jackson Five appeared on TV's "The Hollywood Palace," on October 18, 1969, with Diana Ross and the Supremes. The youngsters were irresistibly charming. Jackie was 18; Tito was 16; Jermaine was 15; Marlon was 12; and Michael was 11 years old.

Two months later, to the day, Motown released *Diana Ross Presents the Jackson Five*. Two million copies sold within months! The timing was perfect—again managed by Berry Gordy and his people at Motown.

In January 1970 Diana Ross officially broke from the Supremes to become a solo performer. She became the star in the Motown crown. Everything she touched seemed to sparkle. It was no accident that Motown closely identified the Jackson Five with Diana Ross. It was a good match, and not just for business. They really enjoyed working together.

Diana and Michael complemented each other on stage. Diana was flashy and dramatic. Michael was young, lively, and full of enthusiasm. Both possessed the vitality and confidence that made them totally entertaining. To some it was shocking to see how much Michael resembled Diana. They could easily pass for mother and son; in fact, there was a rumor circulating at one time that she was his mother. They aren't even distantly related.

In early 1970 the catchy *ABC* album was released by Motown, and by March 14, 1970, it was at the top of the charts. The album went solid gold, and by the end of 1970 the group had four number-one singles, four albums, and a Grammy Award for "ABC" as the best pop song of the year.

The Jackson Five was the hottest group in Motown history. Now they had their own Midas touch. Everything they sang turned to gold—or platinum. Berry Gordy was excited about the new Motown sound and labeled it "soul bubble gum." He explained, "It's a style that appeals to the

By 1972 the Jacksons were featured on TV shows, such as the "Sonny and Cher Comedy Hour."

younger teens. We provide total guidance. We provide their materials, set their music basic sound and work out the choreographic routines."

It was either a brilliant move on the part of Motown or it was a stroke of luck. The Jackson Five filled a void in the record industry. The ten-to-fourteen-year-olds—the bubble-gum set—were consumers who would buy, and buy often, if they liked the sound. The sound had to be crisp with a good dance beat. The lyrics had to appeal to their interests.

By 1971 the bubble-gum sound was a blockbuster. Fans all over the country were caught up in Jacksonmania. And Motown sold their image. Jackie, Tito, Jermaine, Marlon, and Michael were well-mannered kids from middle America; they were from a two-parent family in which high moral standards prevailed. The public loved it.

Joe and Katherine were concerned about the effects of this instant success on

All ages were fascinated by the sounds and moves of the Jackson Five. Performing before the viewers of "Soul Train" boosted their popularity.

their sons. "We just didn't let them run wild," Joe Jackson has said repeatedly. Katherine was just as strict in her own loving way. Both parents were concerned that money, fame, and fortune might go to their sons' heads. The Jacksons tried to protect their sons—some say they were overprotective—to shield them from the pitfalls of stardom. Since Michael was the youngest, he received a double portion of that watchful care.

The group kept moving up. On September 19, 1971, the Jackson Five special, "Goin' Back to Indiana," was aired on ABC. Mayor Hatcher, who had known the young performers before they were famous, proudly announced that "the Jackson Five has carried the name of Gary throughout the country and the world and made it a name to be proud of."

By the end of 1971 the Jacksons had cut three more albums and had three more hit singles. They did other TV specials and were even featured in a weekly animated cartoon series.

Motown recording stars had previously been slotted as black performers who had a predominantly black audience. With the Jacksons, Berry Gordy had proved that Motown could compete with the large white recording studios. The Jackson Five was a favorite with both black and white teenagers. They were a perfect crossover group.

By the spring of 1972, the bubble-gum sound was a real success. There were still a few doubting Thomases who wouldn't believe that the group had any staying power. Some of these early critics of the bubble-gum sound saw it as a fad. They said that the Jackson brothers, and other groups like them, would blaze hot for a short time and then cool down and die out. The predictions were that when Jackie and Tito became interested in girls and Michael's voice changed, that would be the end of the Jackson Five and their sound. Those doomsayers were in for a big surprise. The Jacksons changed but they did not end.

Chapter 3
THOSE JACKSON BROTHERS

By 1972 Michael and his brothers were the most popular males in show business. Everybody wanted to know about them—what they were really like. Ten years after they soared to the top of the record charts, fans were still trying to find out about the private Jacksons.

In the early days, Sigmund Esco Jackson (Jackie) was often called the "old man" of the group; he is the oldest Jackson brother. Born May 4, 1951, he was twenty-one years old in 1972. Girls swooned when they learned that Jackie was also an athlete who had originally planned to pursue a career in professional baseball. When the Jackson brothers became successful in music, Jackie accepted his destiny. But today he still enjoys a good game of baseball and attends baseball games when he isn't performing.

Jackie's older-brother image was particularly evident during the early stages of the Jackson Five's career. During interviews, it was Jackie who answered most of the questions. It was Jackie who kept his younger brothers, Marlon and Michael, in line. According to Joe, Jackie wanted rehearsals to move quickly and smoothly,

In November, 1972, the "Jackson Family Musical Hour" aired on CBS Sunday nights. (Left to right are Tito, Marlon, Michael, Jackie, Jermaine.)

with no playing around. Jackie was strictly for business.

Teenagers were always interested in knowing whom the Jackson brothers were dating. For a while Jackie dated Debracca Foxx, daughter of Redd Foxx, star of "Sanford and Son," a popular TV show. But it was Enid Spann who became Mrs. Sigmund Jackson, on November 24, 1974. The couple were married in Las Vegas in a very informal ceremony. In fact, Jackie is said to have worn tennis shoes.

Enid and Jackie have one son, Sigmund II, who was born in 1977. Although Enid is a busy wife and mother, she is also a businesswoman. She owns a boutique that creates fashions for stage performers —including her famous husband and brothers-in-law.

Remembering the early days when the J-5 were the teenage craze, Jackie has said, "Everybody was looking at the younger guys, I guess. Maybe I'm wrong. But, I didn't care; I was just happy being in the group...." The word that best describes Jackie is *cooperative*. The color that best reflects his character is a calming blue.

Jackie is a Taurus whose zodiac symbol is the bull, but it is his brother Toriano Adryll [Tito] whose name means "the bull." And Tito, the second Jackson son, born October 15, 1953, is bullish when it comes to mastering something he starts. It is Tito who sets the rhythmic sound of the Jacksons on his guitar.

In appearance Tito is more like his father than any of his brothers. He has strong features and is built like a linebacker. The word *self-assured* best describes Tito and his color is orange.

In the early days Tito gained a reputation for being a strong, silent type. His brothers see him as the quiet achiever. There was never a lot of fanfare around Tito, but his accomplishments are numerous. He is a songwriter, a producer, and has, through the years, earned a reputation for being one of the finest guitarists in the business. He unwinds by tinkering with antique cars when he isn't on tour with his famous family.

When Tito was eighteen he married his high school sweetheart, DeeDee. At the time many people predicted that the marriage wouldn't last. But it has. Tito and DeeDee have three children, Taj, Tarryl, and Tito Joe.

Jermaine is the third son of Joe and Katherine Jackson. When the Jackson Five first roared onto the scene, it was Jermaine who captured the hearts of the teenaged girls. At the time Michael and Marlon were too young, but Jermaine was just right. He has often been described as warm, gentle, and very soulful. His smile has won fans for him all over the world.

The word that seems to be applied most often to Jermaine is *sensitive,* although in the early days he had a reputation for being flashy. He also was a real charmer. Who could stay angry with a guy who had a smile like Jermaine's?

In 1973 when he was eighteen, Jermaine commented, "I'm happy, but I'm not happy, happy. I'm only fair happy...." At the time there were millions of girls who would have loved to try to remedy that situation. But before the year was over, Jeramine had reached a decision. He asked Hazel Gordy, the daughter of Berry Gordy, Jr., to be his wife.

Their December wedding has been described as an exercise in extravagance. But Berry Gordy offered no excuses for spending an estimated $200,000 on his daughter's wedding. Hazel was his only daughter, he had the means, and it was his privilege to give his daughter a wedding in whatever style he chose.

Some of the biggest celebrities in show business attended the lavish affair. Gordy escorted his daughter down the aisle. She wore a bridal gown that had a twelve-foot train, lined in white mink and decorated with 7,500 hand-sewn pearls. Smokey Robinson sang a love song that he wrote especially for the occasion.

Jermaine waited for his bride at the altar, dressed in a classic white tuxedo. This was a little bit out of character for the young man who had through the years gained the reputation of being the flashiest dresser of the Jackson brothers. He was known for his far-out styles and his huge flip-flop hats. But on his wedding day, Jermaine chose to be elegant. And he was.

With the marriage of Hazel and Jermaine, the relationship between the Jackson Five and Motown seemed assured of remaining on solid footing. But two years later, Jermaine was faced with one of the toughest decisions he would ever

The marriage of Hazel Gordy and Jermaine Jackson strained the business relationship between the Motown family and the Jacksons.

have to make. His brothers were leaving Motown. After giving the matter a lot of consideration, Jermaine decided to stay at Motown as a solo artist. For a while his decision strained the relationship between him and his brothers and, even more so, with his father. Joe Jackson would not easily forgive the maverick son who dared to defy him.

The battle between Motown and the Jackson Five put Hazel Gordy Jackson right in the middle. There was a great deal of speculation about why the Jackson family wanted to leave Motown and why Jermaine wanted to stay. But it is Hazel's answer to her husband that put their marriage in its proper perspective. "I asked her," said Jermaine, "if I go with my brothers, will that have anything to do with our relationship? She answered, 'No, we're married and in love, not married and in business.'"

While at Motown, Jermaine teamed with Stevie Wonder to produce *Let's Get Serious*. It established him as a star in his own right. This independent success served as the foundation upon which a reconciliation could be built.

Jermaine is a vegetarian. He loves horses and has owned as many as twenty-five horses at a time. He lives with his wife, Hazel, and two children, a son and daughter, outside Los Angeles. His color is yellow because he has mellowed through the years.

Marlon David Jackson is only slightly older than his brother Michael. When Marlon and Michael were younger, they were inseparable—best friends as well as brothers—and to a large degree they still are. Michael and Marlon are alike in many ways. Marlon is a very private person who chooses not to be in the limelight. He chose, for example, in 1975, to keep his marriage to Carol Parker a secret. Even Papa Joe didn't know they had been married in August of 1975. It was a full four months before it was officially verified that eighteen-year-old Marlon was married.

Many observers of the Jackson Five believe that being so close to Michael in age and appearance might have been a handicap for Marlon. But Marlon's brothers don't agree. They are quick to point out his contributions. It was Marlon who worked out the group's difficult dance routines in the early years. Today Marlon is also a songwriter and a producer. He and his wife, Carol, have three children and live in California. Marlon's world is stable, and his color is green, the color of the evergreen—fresh and alive.

When Jermaine went solo, the young-

From left to right are Randy, Tito, Jackie, Michael, and Marlon.

est Jackson brother, Steven Randall, better known as "Randy," was added to the group. They then became known as the Jacksons. Fans the world over held their breaths when Randy was in a near-fatal car accident in 1980. At first the doctors thought they would have to amputate both his legs. Even though the amputations proved unnecessary, both legs were paralyzed. It looked as though Randy would spend the rest of his life in a wheelchair. The best word to describe Randy is *determined*. He believed he would walk again. Much to his fans' delight (and his family's too), within a year after his accident, Randy was back performing with his brothers. His color is purple, the color of patience.

Randy is a Scorpio, born October 29, 1961. He is often described as quiet and pleasant. He is a gifted songwriter who co-wrote "Shake Your Body Down" with his brother Michael. Like his older brothers, he is also married and a father.

There are three girls in the Jackson family—Maureen, LaToya and Janet—all strikingly beautiful. Maureen, the oldest, is married and lives in Kentucky with her family. LaToya is pursuing a singing career and recently cut her first album. Janet is an actress; she was a regular on two TV sitcoms—"Good Times" and "Diff'rent

Janet Jackson holds the key to her own success—an acting career.

Following in her brothers' footsteps, LaToya weaves magic from talent and song.

Strokes.'' Janet, too, has cut an album. Neither Janet nor LaToya is married. They live in Encino with their parents.

The Jackson family is well known for their large eyes, creamy milk-chocolate skin, radiant smiles, and close family ties. "They are beautiful people," says Cynthia Horner, editor of *Right On/Class* magazine. In her introduction to the popular book, *Papa Joe's Boys,* by Leonard Pitts, Jr., she wrote: "My first impression of the Jacksons, whom I originally met in 1976, was that they were, indeed, a set of very, very special people, brought into this world by special parents. All of them possess determination, perseverance, and raw talent which has set them head and shoulders above any entertainers who have ever entered the business." From 1970 to today, the Jacksons have had millions of fans who would agree with Cynthia Horner's assessment.

(Above) New Orleans crowds are held spellbound by the lightning-effect of the Jackson experience. (Below) Michael quickly changes into a tuxedo and returns to a New York stage for an encore.

Chapter 4
THE JACKSON/MOTOWN SPLIT

In 1972 Motown had two of the leading vocal acts in the country—Diana Ross and the Jackson Five. Other family groups had sprung up; for example, the Partridge Family and the Osmond Brothers, with little Donny Osmond as their lead singer and Michael's counterpart. The Osmonds and Jacksons shared similar family backgrounds. The only difference, really, was that the Jackson Five were black and the Osmonds were white.

At one time that difference might have meant something, but in the 1970s the world was changing. In the past black artists were never placed in competition with white artists—the music was kept separate. But the old barriers were crumbling. The idea that there was black music and white music was dismissed as myth. And young listeners were asking to hear the Jackson Five on stations that previously had not played soul music.

While the world was changing rapidly, things were happening for the Jackson brothers, too. It was a special time for Michael. In 1972 Motown released Michael's first single, "Ben," the title song from a horror movie about a young man's strange

An early pose of Michael shows how much his style has changed.

friendship with rats—one in particular named Ben. The irony of the song was that Michael, a black child only one step removed from the ghetto, was singing a song of endearment for a rat. Rats are the scourge of ghetto dwellers everywhere! It was hard to listen to the song without either laughing or frowning. But when the initial feelings of amusement or disgust passed, the craftsmanship of Michael's delivery established him as a solo artist of high standard.

The group traveled to India, Japan, Australia, and Africa. Their command performance before the royal family of England was a major success and a memorable experience for everyone. The queen was said to have tapped her foot to the beat, proving that the Jackson brothers "had a beat that couldn't be beat."

The family has never forgotten that first world tour. It was full of wonder and surprises everywhere they went. Their experiences were myriad, and their impact on their audiences was positive and upbeat. The Jacksons were excellent ambassadors of goodwill.

In Africa Michael was deeply touched by the poverty, but he was impressed with the various African cultures. "I always thought that blacks, as far as artistry, were the most talented race on earth," he said "but, when I went to Africa, I was even more convinced. They do incredible things there. They've got the beat and rhythm. I really see where drums come from.... I don't want American blacks ever to forget that this is where we come from and where our music comes from. I want us to remember!" It was this respect for black Africa that caused Michael to cancel a proposed 1979 performance in South Africa.

The mid-70s was a time of discos, flashing lights, wild colors, and energetic dancing. The Jackson Five's hit single, "Dancing Machine," set the disco sound and was one of the most popular dance tunes on the charts.

Meanwhile, Motown was expanding. Berry Gordy's personal management of Diana Ross had landed her a starring role in *Lady Sings the Blues,* the film biography of Billie Holiday. Ross's performance won her an Academy Award nomination for best actress.

In spite of the good things that were happening, by the end of 1973 the trouble between the Jacksons and Motown had begun. Then, in 1974 Joe Jackson accepted an engagement for the group at MGM Grand in Las Vegas without Motown's approval.

The whole Jackson family came to

The Jacksons' variety show aired on television from June to July, 1976. All but Jermaine participated. Pictured are LaToya (right), Randy, Maureen, Michael (back left), Jackie, Marlon, Janet, and Tito.

help make the show a success. Even Maureen, LaToya, and Janet contributed their talents to the act. The Jackson magic worked. They got rave reviews consistently. But Motown was not happy.

Suddenly there were rumors floating from coast to coast. Were the Bubble-gum Babies getting ready to defect? Was there bad blood between Papa Joe and Berry Gordy? For a time all lips were sealed. Motown officials refused to answer any questions regarding the status of the Jackson Five's contract negotiations. Then the news broke—the Jackson Five were leaving Motown and signing with Epic Records. No. Only four were leaving. Jermaine was remaining and going solo. The fans went wild.

Why? What would happen now? Papa Joe defended his management decision. To him it was business, and business had nothing to do with being grateful. For Michael the move meant more creativity. He said, "At Motown we wanted to do our own writing, but that wasn't in our contract, and they wouldn't give it to us. We didn't have publishing rights, either, and we had trouble getting a proper account of our money. Now, we have our own publishing company and we can record anybody we want."

Motown argued that they had invested a considerable amount of money into the grooming of the Jackson Five. They felt that they were justified in trying to recoup on their investment. Motown warned the Jackson Five publicly that Epic was part of the large CBS broadcasting network, and that they would lose the almost familylike togetherness they had shared at Motown. Nor would they get the personalized attention they had been used to.

Papa Joe insisted that it was simply time to move on. And that is what the Jackson Four did—leaving the fifth Jackson, Jermaine, behind. It was a sad time for fans and for the family, as well. Michael missed Jermaine. "Ever since we started singing, Jermaine was in a certain spot near me on stage," he told an interviewer after the split. "All of a sudden he was gone," he said. "It felt bare on that side for a long time."

In time the tensions between the family members eased; hot tempers cooled; love was the salve that healed the wound. But the bitter business battle raged on and on in the courts. Motown sued and won the right to keep the Jackson Five name. The group was renamed the Jacksons, and they never skipped a beat.

In retrospect, the move to Epic proved to be beneficial for the Jacksons. In 1974 they were no longer little boys. While ev-

While on tour in England, the Jacksons made several guest appearances and posed for ads.

erybody was looking at them, Papa Joe's boys had grown up and changed. It was time for their music to change, too.

The Jacksons' fans and critics were in for a surprise. These young men were already ten-year show-business veterans, and they had talent they were just getting ready to use—especially Michael.

Chapter 5
THE SECOND GENERATION

The Jacksons got off to a good start at Epic Records. Kenny Gamble and Leon Huff were the producers of the group's first two albums with the company—*The Jacksons* (1976) and *Goin' Places* (1977).

The second-generation Jacksons were terrific. Many fans were discovering them for the first time; others had followed the group from their early years and had literally grown up listening to the Jacksons' music. They were like a whole new act. Their sound was different. Their concerts were different. But they were as fresh and lively as ever. Everybody knew that these young men were talented and that they were going to be around for a while.

At last the Jacksons had a chance to produce their own album. The *Destiny* album was all theirs, and it went gold and platinum. The Jacksons began the second stage of their careers as number-one recording artists and as credible producers and songwriters. Michael's talents were especially showcased in *Destiny*. Michael and Randy's "Shake Your Body Down" became a hit single and the most requested disco song of 1978.

The Jackson brothers were very proud.

The Jacksons were "Goin' Places" with their newest member, Randy (front). Behind him are Marlon, Tito, Jackie, and Michael.

Their first effort was a family affair. The brothers worked long, hard hours in their Encino studio planning, writing, and working out the details.

Marlon explained: "When we were mixing the album, a lot of people thought each one of us would have a knob on the board. But we outslicked all of them. We'd send maybe Tito and Michael in to mix it down, and the rest of us would sit out and wait until they'd get the mix. Then fresh ears would come in and listen to it, because once you keep hearing the song over and over you lose something. The next song, somebody else would mix down."

On the back of the cover of *Destiny* is a peacock. It has symbolic meaning, which Michael explained: The peacock is the only bird that blends all the colors of the rainbow into one. It radiates this wonderful color when it is in love. "And that is what we are trying to do with our music," said Michael at the time, "...to bring all races together through love. The significance is important to me and is one of the main reasons I do what I do. If I couldn't bring happiness to people all over the world through music, I wouldn't do it. I could never just make records for people to buy and just get rich from."

At the peak of the *Destiny* success in 1979, the Jacksons had to cancel seven performances on their tour. Michael's voice just gave out. All he could do was croak and squeak. Rest was prescribed. Michael was physically drained. But even while he was recuperating, Michael's mind was at work planning his new solo album.

Whatever Michael Jackson does and says is very important. Unfortunately, for a while, whatever he said was misquoted, misunderstood, or falsified. As a result, Michael became very guarded in public and limited his interviews. But his self-imposed isolation had exactly the opposite effect. Instead of being left alone, Michael became more sought after than ever. The less people knew about him, the more they wanted to know. What they couldn't find out about they guessed—and very often those guesses were wrong.

Michael knows that he lives in a glass house and has said, "My biggest fear is of being misquoted. One word can be cut into a statement and change the complete meaning and coloring of what was meant."

In spite of all the personal ups and downs, Michael Jackson entered the 1980s as a superstar. The 1980s would see still another generation of Jackson rhythms, lyrics, and dance steps.

Chapter 6
EASING ON DOWN THE ROAD

Michael loves movies—old movies, new movies, cartoons, drama, comedy—he loves them all. He also loves acting, not on stage but on the silver screen. "Whatever we do on stage is just for the people in the audience at that moment—what about the miltitude of people who aren't there? But, if you can capture it on film, then it's forever."

Michael got his first taste of acting when he was cast as the Scarecrow in the 1977 movie version of *The Wiz*. *The Wiz* was the successful Broadway play that had won the Tony Award. With the very popular and talented Diana Ross starring as Dorothy, backed up by veteran actors and actresses such as Ted Ross as the Cowardly Lion, Nipsey Russell as the Tin Man, Mabel King as the Wicked Witch Evilene, Richard Pryor as the Wiz, and Lena Horne as the Good Witch Glinda, the movie, directed by Sidney Lumet, should have been a box office bonanza. But it wasn't. Even the name of the genius Quincy Jones, the musical director on the project, didn't help the film get the reviews the producer had hoped.

The movie was panned by movie crit-

Playing the Scarecrow in the film version of the Broadway play The Wiz *meant magic and fantasy for Michael (right). In his first film appearance, he worked alongside such creative artists as Diana Ross (center) and Nipsey Russell (left).*

ics. They said it was overproduced and poorly cast. Some people think of Dorothy as a teenager, but the book doesn't mention Dorothy's age. Diana Ross wanted to play the part. She had the voice and the dancing ability, but she was well over thirty-two years of age. So, her producers rewrote the script, which cast her as a twenty-four-year-old schoolteacher. But the critics wouldn't accept this interpretation.

Within the black community, however, the movie was proudly received as a welcome relief. At last there was a movie a black family could attend, a movie with no pimps, hustlers, dope addicts, or con artists. There were positive images of black people and a cheerful uplifting plot. It was quite a contrast from some of the materials being presented on television and other media presentations featuring black people. The film's artistic merits were not questioned as the all-black cast danced and sang across the screen with breathtaking energy and vitality. In the dramatic climax, when Lena Horne sang "If You Believe," she made believers out of millions of children. Her encouraging words were, "Believe in yourself...as I believe in you."

Michael is a believer. He says so himself. "I love acting so much," he has said many times. "It's fun, it's just neat to become another thing, another person. Especially when you really believe it and it's not like you're acting. I always hated the word *acting*. Or 'I'm an actor.' It should be more like, 'I'm a believer.'"

Just weeks before rehearsals were to begin on *The Wiz*, Michael became ill again. It was the Fourth of July, 1977, and he was at the beach. Suddenly he couldn't breathe and had to be rushed to the hospital. He was diagnosed as having pneumothorax—bubbles in the lungs that burst and make it hard to breathe. It usually happens to very thin people. At the time Michael weighed only 115 pounds. He began eating everything, trying to gain weight and strength. Nothing seemed to work. Was he going to miss out on his life's dream?

Michael believed he was supposed to play that part and he was at rehearsals when they started in August. He turned nineteen during the second week of rehearsals. This was his first time away from home all by himself. LaToya came to stay with him. Michael does not like to be alone.

Filmmaking fascinated Michael from the start. He wanted to learn everything he could and having Sidney Lumet as a director was a good way to start. As a beginning actor, Michael listened to Lumet's directions carefully and followed them to the letter. According to the famous director, Michael has the potential for becoming a fine actor—with natural talent.

Every day Michael discovered something new. It was all a learning process—the staging, the lighting, everything. For example, he had had no idea how long it took to put on makeup and prepare for the actual filming. Then there was set design, costuming, and so much more. Once Michael got the hang of things, he became totally absorbed in the part and very often forgot to remove his makeup.

Working on *The Wiz* was a personal accomplishment for Michael. It was the first time he had performed in a role that showed his real acting ability. He said at the time, "This is my first acting role. I mean, I've been in movies before, but they were concert-type films like *Save the Children*. This is my first time I played a part instead of just being myself...it was one of my dreams come true."

The film was produced during one of the coldest winters in New York history. Michael recalled, "We worked outside a lot; it was cold, the coldest ever in New York. There were six hundred dancers at the World Trade Center, all wearing costumes like swim outfits, and it was so cold

Michael flashes a childlike smile at the 1978 opening of The Wiz.

a lot of them quit...." But Michael was charged with excitement; he didn't mind the cold.

Scarecrow is a memorable character in *The Wiz*. In his first scene he is seen stuck on a pole; his head is stuffed full of garbage—not straw. Michael calls attention to this detail. "I watched the old film. I tried not to do it, but then I did watch it on TV a number of times and sometimes I'd turn the sound off and just watch the moves. I hate to say this, but when you watch the old one you realize that they didn't bring out what should have been brought out."

In *The Wiz* Scarecrow is tormented by three negative crows, who do nothing but spread discouragement. "What's the use of tryin'," they croak. Michael's "You Can't Win," written especially for the movie version by Quincy Jones, is one of the most enjoyable songs in the film. Scarecrow, convinced that the crows are right, sings, "You can't win; you can't break even and you can't get out of the game."

Then along comes Dorothy, played by Diana Ross, a withdrawn New York teacher who is on her way to find the Wiz. She shoos the crows away and convinces Michael/Scarecrow that he should come with her to find the Wiz. The Wiz is the one who can help her find her way back home and perhaps can also help the Scarecrow get some brains. Side-by-side Scarecrow and Dorothy follow the yellow brick road that leads to the Emerald City—the home of the mighty Wiz! "Ease On Down the Road" is the wonderfully upbeat tune that is their traveling song. It has become a classic, equal to "We're Off to See the Wizard" from the movie *The Wizard of Oz*.

Both "Ease On Down the Road" and "You Can't Win" were released as singles by MCA. "Ease On Down the Road" made it to number 17 on the Billboard soul charts in October 1978; "You Can't Win" (Part 1) made it to number 42 in January 1979.

On every film set there are off-camera happenings that are sometimes funny, sometimes frightening, but always memorable. Michael shared some of the behind-the-scene moments from *The Wiz*.

There is one scene in which Scarecrow has to catch Dorothy when she faints. Diana was too heavy for Michael, but he huffed and puffed until he got the job done. Nobody realized his problem until it was over. "I just couldn't drop her," he said. "So I hung on."

Another experience was not so funny; in fact, it could have been tragic. Diana

was literally blinded when she looked at the powerful spotlights that were the Wizard's eyes. It was a frightening experience for everyone on the set. Fortunately, the blindness was temporary.

For Michael, the filming of the movie was a wonderful adventure, one he wished could go on forever. He has often told his friends that working on that film was one of the most enjoyable times of his life. Although *The Wiz* didn't get the praise many thought it deserved, Michael made his mark on the movie industry. All his personal reviews were excellent. He promised himself that he would be back again...and again. "I'm serious and sincere about movies. The thing I love about films is that they capture moments that need never be lost and that we can constantly learn from."

From Scarecrow in **The Wiz** *to "a wiz" on the dance floor, Michael does some fancy stepping.*

Chapter 7
MICHAEL AND FRIENDS

Michael once said, "I love experienced people. I love people who are phenomenally talented. I love people who've worked so hard and been so courageous and are the leaders in their fields. For me to meet somebody like that and learn from them and share words with them—to me that's magic. . . ." One has only to look at Michael's list of friends to get the full impact of what he means. Counted among his friends are some of the most talented and experienced people in show business.

There are only a few people who have become friends of this very private person. But those who have find that no one could value a personal relationship more than he. Cynthia Horner, editor of *Right On/Class* magazine, feels that Michael is a "rare and true friend." She continues, "I feel blessed to enjoy a special relationship with this very special man."

As a professional writer, Horner got a clear insight into his life. Michael was shy with her at first, but later they became good buddies. She expresses her feeling about why she thinks her friend is so shy: "How would you feel if you had to stay safely locked behind electronic gates with

Both Diana Ross and Michael hold 1981 American Music Awards: Diana for favorite soul single, "Upside Down," and Michael for favorite soul album, Off the Wall.

fans from all over the world pressing the bell hoping to gain admittance day and night? How would you feel if you tried to go roller-skating with your sisters only to have to flee because people mobbed the car in the parking lot before you could even get near the rink?...I witnessed the above-mentioned situations first-hand, so I empathize with this young performer."

Another friend who is close to Michael and understands him well is actress Jane Fonda. Michael has a great deal of respect for her and they spend hours together talking about everything.

Michael got a chance to visit the set of *On Golden Pond*, starring Henry Fonda, Jane's father, Katharine Hepburn, and Jane herself. Michael met and spent time with Henry Fonda, a very gifted performer, who had been in the business for many years. Fonda died shortly after the film was made. But he lived long enough to know that he had won his first Academy Award for Best Actor for his performance in that film. Michael had seen a piece of film history being made.

Jane observed that Michael and her father shared a common problem—shyness. "Dad was also painfully self-conscious and shy in life, and he really only felt comfortable when he was behind the mask of a character. He could liberate himself only

The commitment and excellence of such classic performers as Katharine Hepburn attract Michael. He admires in others what he strives to attain during his own stage appearances.

when he was being someone else. That's a lot like Michael."

Actress Katharine Hepburn is also counted among Michael Jackson's friends. She, too, is a superstar who has maintained a level of excellence in her work that demands respect. Yet, she is also a very private person. Imagine being coached by Katharine Hepburn! Michael had this rare and wonderful opportunity, and he's never forgotten it. He didn't have to be told how fortunate he was. Michael knew he had the chance of a lifetime.

Michael learns from all his friends, drawing upon their knowledge. But he also gives in his relationships, as is shown in his care and concern for the Fonda family after Henry Fonda died. He knew the tremendous sadness that the Fonda family must have been feeling and was one of the first to visit the family the night Jane's father died.

In 1981, Michael visited Katharine Hepburn in her New York apartment. There she let him share some of her private mementos. Then in September 1981 Ms. Hepburn shocked the world by attending a rock concert at Madison Square Garden. She had gone there to see her friend Michael Jackson and his brothers perform!

It was Ms. Hepburn who asked Michael to remove his dark glasses at the Grammy Awards show in 1984. He acknowledged that she had asked him, and to honor her request, he removed his glasses—even though only for a moment.

Holding six of his eight Grammys, Michael stops briefly backstage to pose with **Menudo,** *a sensational young rock group.*

Liza Minnelli is also high on the Michael Jackson list of favorite people. They talk...and talk...and talk. Liza is the daughter of Judy Garland, the actress who played Dorothy in the original *Wizard of Oz* film. Michael says that he and Liza share a common background—growing up in the glitter and glare of Hollywood. "What I like about Liza is that when we get together it's all talk. I show her my favorite step, and she shows me hers. She's a show-stopping performer, too. She has real charisma."

Then there's Stephanie Mills, the young actress/singer who played Dorothy in the stage version of *The Wiz*. When Michael was filming the movie version, he went to see the play eight times. Many believed he was also going to see Stephanie, and there was talk about there being romantic ties between the two. But Michael maintained that they were just good friends, and they still are.

Another one of Michael's super friends is Steven Spielberg, one of the most brilliant producers/directors in the movie business. In 1982 Michael was asked to record *E.T. the Extra-Terrestrial*, the Quincy Jones-Steven Spielberg storybook record project. Michael jumped at the opportunity. When Michael saw the movie *E.T.*, he says he cried. It was while he sang

Liza Minnelli and Michael share similar childhood backgrounds and rare, natural talent.

Another creative force for Michael is the childlike imagination of Steven Spielberg.

and narrated the story that Michael got to meet one of his all-time favorites, E.T.

"I was actually there," he said after cutting the record. "The next day, I missed him a lot. I wanted to go back to that spot I was at yesterday in the forest. I wanted to be there."

Spielberg has said, "If E.T. hadn't come to Elliott, he would have come to Michael's house." Spielberg considers Michael "one of the last living innocents who is in complete control of his life. I've never seen anybody like Michael. He's an emotional star child."

Maybe that's why Michael loves children and being around them so much. "Another inspiration for me, and I don't know where it came from, is children. If I'm down I'll take a book with children's pictures and look at it and it will just lift me up. Being around children is magic .... When I'm upset... I'll dash off on my bike and ride to a schoolyard, just to be around them. When I come back to the studio, I'm ready to move mountains. Kids do that to me. It's like magic."

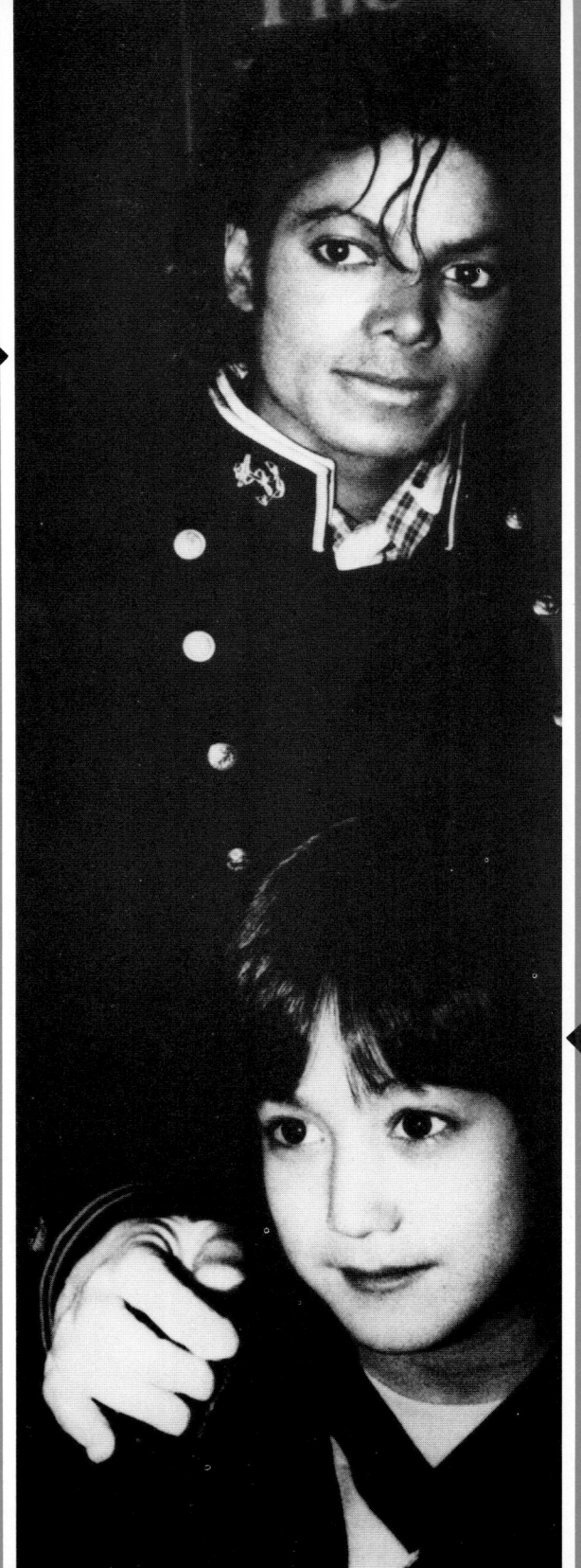

After attending a performance of The Tap Dance Kid *at the Broadhurst Theater in New York, Michael spends time with Sean Lennon, son of the late John Lennon.*

During a 1981 performance at Madison Square Garden, Michael is unaware that a very special friend sits in the audience—Katharine Hepburn.

Michael shares the stage with Lionel Richie during the 1984 American Music Awards. Michael would have made a clean sweep of the awards if it were not for Richie's award for "All Night Long."

The special love Michael has for children can only be matched by his love for animals. "I'm a sucker for animals," he says. He does have an unusual assortment of animal friends that share his home in Encino. It's like a mini-zoo. He has a boa constrictor named Muscles and a llama named Louis. The llama, which came from a traveling circus, can do tricks. His zoo also has a sheep named Mr. Tibbs, two deer, two dogs, a cat, and cockatoo parrots. (One of the most popular posters of Michael shows him posing with one of his cockatoos.)

Michael's inquisitive mind is always

alert and ready to gather new information. He likes to observe his animals. "I think they're sweet..." he says, then adds, "I like to pry into their world and watch the way they move about. I just stare at them."

In Michael's life there is one person whose friendship means even more to him than all others—Diana Ross. For nearly fifteen years they have been closely linked in their personal and private lives. There is no doubt in his mind that he loves her. Once when asked whom he would marry —he answered, "Diana Ross."

Bob Giraldi, a video director for both performers, says, "They have a friendship as genuine as any I've seen. On the set Diana would say, 'What would Michael think of this?' Michael would say, 'What would Diana do with this?'"

As close as they are, even she is unable to get him to come more out of himself. She told *Rolling Stone* magazine that her friend "spends a lot of time—too much time—to himself.... Michael has a lot of people around him, but he's afraid...."

With all the wonderful people he has around him he's still a lonely person. But he opens up when he is performing. "On stage I feel safe. If I could I would sleep on the stage. I'm serious."

Jane Fonda says, "In some ways Michael reminds me of the walking wounded. He's an extremely fragile person." Those who know and love him the most know how true that is.

Animals hold a special place in the Jackson home. Michael caresses a pet dove, then poses with his brothers and their favorite dogs in the yard of their California home.

(Left) After being honored with a special award of merit during the 11th Annual American Music Awards, Michael receives a kiss from Diana.

Chapter 8
TWO GENIUSES

Michael's love of fantasy, his wide-eyed enthusiasm, and his constant search for the wonder and surprise in the world might lead some people to believe he is childish. Quite the opposite. Michael Jackson is a smart businessman. Nobody controls his life or his work. With more than fifteen years of show-business experience behind him, he knows how to make decisions and how to achieve his goals.

One wise decision that Michael made was to produce a solo album. He called on another good friend, Quincy Jones, to help him produce it. That proved to be one of the smartest moves Michael ever made; Quincy Jones is a musical genius.

"Q," as he is called by people close to him, began his musical career as a trumpeter in the 1950s. During his seven years with Mercury Records, he produced music for a number of well-known vocal and instrumental artists. Since that time, Jones has earned a reputation for being one of the most prolific, but consistently good, producers, arrangers, conductors, and composers on the scene. His credits include the theme songs for television series

Quincy Jones shares the spotlight with Michael after being honored as Producer of the Year at the 1984 Annual Grammy Awards.

such as "Sanford and Son" and Alex Haley's "Roots," which was serialized on ABC in 1977. He has also written music for well over fifty movies.

It was on the set of *The Wiz* that Michael Jackson first met the legendary Quincy Jones. They liked working with each other, and each was impressed with the other's abilities. They both wanted to do more work together; it was just a matter of time. Michael's timing couldn't have been better than when he decided to give his friend a call to ask about a producer: "After we finished *The Wiz,* I called Quincy Jones to ask if he knew any great producers for my album...." said Michael. Quincy responded, "I tell you what... why don't you let me do it?" The creative genius of Jackson and Jones created the record-breaking album *Off the Wall.*

Another decision Michael made was to work with Paul McCartney. One night at a party at the McCartneys' house, Linda, Paul's wife, told Michael that they had written a song for him, "Girlfriend." They sang it for him right there on the spot. Michael loved it. The song was included in the *Off the Wall* lineup of super hits. The full impact of the McCartney and Jackson musical collaboration would not be felt until later.

Off the Wall went gold and platinum all over the world. It also set a record in that four of the singles made it to the top ten: "Don't Stop 'Til You Get Enough," written by Michael Jackson; "Rock With You," written by Red Temperton; "Off the Wall," written by Red Temperton; and "She's Out of My Life," written by Tom Bahler. Each of the singles was certified gold, and Michael won three awards at the American Music Awards presentation in January 1980: Favorite Male Soul Vocalist, Favorite Soul Album, and Favorite Single for "Don't Stop 'Til You Get Enough." He also won a Grammy for Best Male R&B Vocal Performance for "Don't Stop..." In total *Off the Wall* sold five million copies in the United States and eight million worldwide.

Working with Quincy Jones proved to be a windfall. Michael thoroughly enjoyed the relationship the two shared: "...Working with Quincy was really great. He's wonderful in how he deals with you. He's not selfish in the studio. In other words, he wants you to share your ideas."

Just as soon as *Off the Wall* became a smash hit, the Jacksons released their second self-produced album, *Triumph.* Four singles from it were certified platinum: "Can You Feel It?," "Walk Right Now,"

"Lovely One," and "Heartbreak Hotel."

In 1981 the Jacksons went on tour. There was a lot of speculation that Michael was getting ready to leave the group. Michael told a reporter from the *Los Angeles Times,* "This is my last tour. I love being on stage, but I don't like the other things that go with touring. I didn't even want to do this tour. It was going to be canceled except that we wanted to do the benefit for the children in Atlanta."

During that time, black children in Atlanta, Georgia were being mysteriously murdered. At Michael's request most of the money from the Jacksons' two shows there—more than $250,000—was slated to go to Atlanta's poor families. The murders bothered Michael particularly feeling as he does about children: "They are more than just children. I feel like they are all little geniuses and that they have a secret all their own, a secret they cannot always express. . . . I kind of think they lose it as they get older."

The tour ended. Michael was exhausted. But it wasn't long before the creative juices started to flow again, and he and Quincy were back at the drawing board. What could they possibly do to match *Off the Wall*? Easy . . . just produce a *Thriller!*

Michael shows off the gold records he received for his 1979 album Off the Wall. *Thirteen million copies were sold.*

Chapter 9

THE MAGIC OF *THRILLER*

◆━━━━━━━━━━━━━━━◆

One of Michael's favorite words is *magic*. He uses it to express the feeling he gets when something very special has happened to him. Everything associated with the *Thriller* album has to be labeled MAGIC! It revolutionized the recording industry and added a new dimension to the way people listen to music.

Thriller, like most projects, began with an idea. Michael and Quincy had worked so well on *Off the Wall* that they decided to give their partnership an instant replay. They began by selecting the right songs. Red Temperton's "Thriller" became the title song of the album; it was both fun and unique. Michael hadn't done anything like it before, and he was fascinated by its potential. He and Quincy added all the elements of a horror movie —squeaking doors, wolf howls, and a horror rap by the prince of ghouls, Vincent Price.

"Human Nature," written by John Bettis and Steve Porcaro, was then added to the *Thriller* lineup of songs. Next, Michael and Paul McCartney put their heads together and came up with "The Girl Is Mine." (They also recorded two other

Michael performs on videotape—the song "Beat It" from the **Thriller** *album.*

songs, "Say, Say, Say" and "The Man" for McCartney's album, *Tug of War.*) Add "Billie Jean," written by Michael, and "Beat It," "Wanna Be Startin' Something," and "P.Y.T." (Pretty Young Thing) by Quincy Jones and you've got *Thriller,* the album that was number one for thirty-three weeks.

Thriller was released in December 1982 just in time for Christmas sales. By the New Year it was already number nine on the charts and it stayed in the top ten for the whole year of 1983. *Variety Magazine* said of it, "Jackson reworks familiar romantic themes with his sky-walking falsetto and deliciously stylish delivery...." The *New York Times* critic wrote, "*Thriller* suggests that Jackson's evolution as an artist is far from finished. He is, after all, only twenty-four years old." *Thriller* clearly was a success.

By March 5, 1983, Michael Jackson became the first black artist to have both an album and a single in the number-one spot in the United States and Great Britian.

Then along came MTV (Music TV), a cable network television channel. MTV started a revolution in the way music is presented on TV. It developed a format that features live dramatic performances by recording artists, videotaped for presentation on TV. For the first time, fans

TV mini-musicals provided Michael with a new opportunity—the chance to captivate audiences with his magnetic dance style. The publicity created a dance craze that spread worldwide.

could see their favorite recording stars as they performed their hit songs. These mini-musicals set the stage for Michael to showcase his acting and dancing talents. His hit singles from the *Thriller* album, "Beat It" and "Billie Jean," seemed perfect for the mini-musicals. CBS put up the money and Michael's first two videos were put into production.

Bob Giraldi was selected as the director on both projects. They used actual gang members from the Los Angeles area to make "Beat It." Without being preachy about it, Michael made the point that gangland wars are senseless and a waste of human potential. The "Billie Jean" video is also spirited and charged with excitement. The visual images enhance the lyrics, and Michael's movements are fantastic.

But it was the "Thriller" video that elevated the quality of this new medium and gave it a standard of professionalism that was not present in the industry's first efforts. "Thriller" is like a mini-movie, complete with characterization, setting, and storyline. By December 1983, the videodisc and tape versions of *The Making of Thriller* were released for home viewing. The tape contains the complete video, plus a detailed tour of the behind-the-camera filming of "Thriller."

The tape begins with the credits: "The Thriller" in dripping blood-red letters, starring Michael Jackson, Ola Ray, and directed by John Landis. In the first scene, a 1957 Chevy coughs to a stop in a wooded area. Two young people (Michael and Ola) are seen walking along a deserted road. The couple stops and Michael asks Ola to be his girl. Then he tells her that he's not like other guys. Ola blushes and says, "I know. That's why I love you."

Just as Michael is about to tell her something more, the full moon comes out from behind the clouds. Michael looks up at it; his body begins to tremble. He manages to yell a warning, "Run!" Too late! The metamorphosis has started. Ola screams. Michael changes into a hideous werewolf. Ola runs, but she stumbles and falls. As she lies faceup, the monster leans over her with claws and fangs showing. More screams are heard.

The screams are coming from Ola, only now she is seeing all this in a movie. She tells Michael, her date, that she can't look anymore, and she leaves. Michael is enjoying the horror movie, but he reluctantly follows her. Outside the movie, Michael teases her about being frightened.

As they walk along a deserted street, Michael sings "Thriller." Then the camera cuts to a graveyard. While Vincent Price talks, zombies, ghouls, and vampires crawl out of graves in the foggy cemetery. Their bodies are decaying, and the flesh on their faces is falling off, leaving only bulging eyes and exposed skulls. Ola and Michael seem unaware that they are being stalked by these night creatures, until it's too late! Without warning the couple is surrounded by the walking dead.

Ola screams again. Suddenly Michael is one of the monsters. And he's dancing with them—a delightful fiendish routine. Ola runs into a boarded-up mansion. The monsters follow her, led by Michael, who has superhuman strength. Ola screams and screams. The monsters are coming through the windows, crashing through the walls. Michael breaks down the door and throws it aside. Ola can't look at the horror that is coming toward her. She hides her face just as Michael/Monster is about to grab her. Then suddenly it's OK. It's only Michael. They are safe inside a well-lighted house. It was all just Ola's imagination. Michael takes her hand and they prepare to leave. He looks over his shoulder and there's a demonic glare in his eye. Was it or was it not just Ola's imagination?

The second part of the tape deals with how the film was made from a technical point of view. John Landis, the director, talks about how certain special effects were achieved. Rick Baker, better known as the "monster maker," changes Michael into the werewolf step by step. Michael Peters also tells how he worked with Michael and the dancers on the special choreography. In every respect the entire project was magic!

Also on the tape are exerpts from the "Beat It," "Billie Jean," and "Say, Say, Say" videotapes; the opening video of the Jacksons' concert; early home movies of Michael and his brothers; and Michael's performance of "Billie Jean" at the 1983 Motown Special.

The *Thriller* album and five of the singles won more than thirty-seven awards around the globe. At the 1984 Grammy Awards ceremony, Michael won a total of eight Grammys, which earned him a place in the *Guinness Book of Records*. What will Michael do next?

Confetti falls everywhere as dancers surround Michael at the New York Museum of Natural History. CBS honored Michael for his successful Thriller *album.*

Chapter 10
THE LOOK

In 1970 the Jackson Five set a trend in teenage dressing and dancing. The Jackson brothers wore large well-shaped Afro hairdos, flashy shirts, bell-bottomed trousers, fringed leather/suede vests, and beads. That was the "in" look then.

In the 1980s Michael Jackson is again a trendsetter. From his hair to his dancing shoes, he is the most copied star in the country. Hair stylists report that the "Michael Jackson" hairstyle is the most requested; retailers can't keep white socks in stock, and some fans who want to achieve the total Michael "look" have paid as much as $150 for "the glove."

Offstage Michael is not interested in clothes. He chooses comfort over style. But, onstage he cares a lot. The onstage Michael wears fantastic costumes that have been reproduced and sold for up to as much as $1,000. Copies of the red leather jacket that he wore in the "Thriller" video are being reproduced and marketed for $550 each. Even a leather-look imitation is being sold for $150 and up.

Michael began to change his "image" after *Off the Wall* was produced. He changed his whole outward appearance.

Michael's hairstyle is most often copied by fans who want to achieve the "look" with the least expense. Even so, hair stylists report that the "Jackson Look" hairstyle can cost anywhere from a modest $30 all the way up to $200.

A person who has been closely associated with the Jackson image in clothing is Jill Klien. She is the talented young designer who was responsible for Michael's clothes in "Beat It" and "Billie Jean." She has also worked with Lionel Richie and Kenny Rogers on their videos.

Jill helps Michael find crests, which he collects. He wears them on his shirts, jackets, and sweaters. During an interview, Jill had this to say about Michael: "He talks to you as if what you're doing is just as special as what he's doing, and I really get that from Michael. He respects everyone as an artist. I couldn't say enough good things about Michael Jackson. He's really a pleasure. He gets as much a kick out of what I'm doing as I do from him. It's a nice twist. There's no attitude with Michael...."

Another element of Michael's stage look is the "glove." The idea seems to have originated with him and there is no real explanation for his using just one glove. It has become a part of the Jackson Look and fans are paying as much as $150

Michael performs during a TV special titled: "1983: A Year of Black Achievement."

for a jeweled glove... that has no mate.

Part of Michael's whole image is his style of dancing. His routines are always exciting to watch. On the Motown television special, Michael's performance of "Billie Jean" brought the crowd to its feet and earned him still another honor—an Emmy Award nomination. He didn't win, but he won the praise of Fred Astaire, one of America's leading dancers and a favorite of Michael's. Astaire called the day after the performance to tell Michael how much he enjoyed his dancing.

For a long time Michael had been studying Fred Astaire's dancing style on video—stopping and starting the tapes, watching every muscle. To be recognized by a professional like Astaire was a great honor. Astaire's phone call was a special kind of award.

Another person who has had a part in developing Michael's dance image is Michael Peters, a choreographer. In 1982, Peters won a Tony Award for his work on the Broadway musical *Dream Girls,* which some people insist is about the Supremes, although everyone connected with the show says it is not. (Diana Ross refuses to see the stage play, but Michael has seen the musical many, many times.)

Peters says, "Michael is what I consider a dancer in his soul. He has never

Inspired by the style and grace of Fred Astaire, Michael blends carefully choreographed steps with natural ability. The result is spontaneous eruption of talent.

studied...he's not a professionally trained dancer. He never took dance lessons." Peters worked with Michael on the "Beat It" and "Thriller" videos. "Michael is an incredible performer," says Peters. "It's sort of nitpicking to go on about his lack of formal dance training. If you were to ask anybody in the world if they thought Michael Jackson was a great dancer, they'd say, 'Yes,' and he is!"

Peters is right about that. There are very few dancers who can accomplish Michael's moves with such ease. *Rolling Stone* wrote: "He can tuck his long thin frame into a figure skater's spin without benefit of ice skates. Aided by the burn and flash of silvery body suits, he seems to change molecular structure at will..."

Another part of Michael's image depends on with whom he is seen. Michael doesn't do a lot of dating, but he has taken out a number of very popular Hollywood stars. A few years ago, Michael dated Tatum O'Neal, daughter of Ryan O'Neal. She and her father had starred in *Paper Moon*, which launched her acting career at age ten. Michael enjoyed Tatum's company; they had a lot in common.

Michael has also dated Stephanie Mills and more recently, Brooke Shields. Michael met Brooke at a Hollywood gathering, and they liked each other very much.

Brooke Shields joins Michael at the CBS party to celebrate his success.

They found that they were able to talk, and she has been Michael's guest at several public functions.

Put the clothing, the hairstyle, the moves, and the beautiful girls together, and the public Michael Jackson becomes someone special. Take away the clothing, the hairstyle, the moves, and the beautiful girls, and you have another Michael Jackson—the private Michael Jackson, who is just as special in his faded jeans and plaid shirt.

Michael walks to the White House with President Reagan after receiving an award for participating in a campaign against drunk driving.

Chapter 11
OFF-STAGE WITH MICHAEL

Michael loves the stage. He loves performing. "I have always enjoyed the feeling of being on stage—the magic that comes. When I hit the stage, it's like all of a sudden a magic from somewhere just comes and the spirit just hits you and you just lose control of yourself...."

But, once the stage lights are turned off and the cheering and screaming fans go home and Michael goes to his home in Encino, what does he do? What does he like? Everybody knows the public Michael. His fans can tell you how many Grammy Awards he's won and the exact dates of his upcoming concerts, but they don't know the offstage Michael. Very few people do. But from time to time he has given us a glimpse of his private world.

Outside the Jackson's home in Encino, California, fans sit by the gate hoping to see Michael, or maybe his sisters, his brothers, his parents. The Jacksons rarely permit a tour of their home, but in 1984 *Time* magazine reporter Denise Worrell was invited to view Michael's world from the inside.

According to Worrell's description,

Relaxing at his home in Encino, California gives Michael time to reflect on his career. In private Michael is quiet and shy.

Curious fans stop by the Jackson home to catch a glimpse of their rock idols.

the house is large and beautiful. Room by room she described the furnishings and the color scheme. According to Worrell, off the entrance hall is a trophy room that contains all the Jackson family gold and platinum records. Next to that is a screening room that seats thirty-two. It is decorated in shades of blue. The most striking feature of the den is the large bar that houses an old-fashioned soda fountain. The living room is decorated in floral prints that are on the fabric of the couches, chairs, and rugs.

The estate has a pond with swans and a huge swimming pool. Over the garage is a picture gallery of the Jackson family. Michael loves fantasy and one of the rooms in the house was decorated by Disney Productions. There is also a game room that is lined with all kinds of video games.

Michael's room is on the second floor, along with those of his sisters and parents. It is reported that he spends a lot of time in his room watching old Disney cartoons. He never tires of them; he has seen some of them fifty times or more.

Another outlet for his artistic expression is drawing and painting. "I love to draw—pencil, ink, pen—I love art," he says.

Michael also enjoys reading. He reads all kinds of books. Some of his favorites include *The Red Balloon* by Albert Lamorisse, *Rip Van Winkle* by Washington Irving, *The Complete Works of O. Henry* by O. Henry, and *Abraham Lincoln* by Carl Sandburg.

"I love to read. I like philosophy and short stories," he says. "I like to keep up with the latest best-sellers. The Calendar section in the LA Sunday *Times* is my favorite. I have my favorite authors—it's not like I just read the best-sellers. I like to see what they are doing and keep up with what people are interested in."

Aside from reading and painting, Michael practices his dancing. He practices for thirty minutes without stopping every Sunday. Also he doesn't eat solid food on Sunday; he just drinks juices. "It flushes out the system," he says, "cleans out the colon. I think that's great...."

In Michael's offstage time, he also studies the styles and techniques of people he admires. His list is long. People from various time periods and various areas of the performing arts have been an inspiration to him.

It is no secret that Michael has been greatly influenced by Charlie Chaplin. "The little tramp, the whole gear and everything, and his heart—everything he portrayed on the screen was a truism. It was his whole life.... He roamed the

Snow White and Dopey pay a visit to Michael and present him with a one-of-a-kind display featuring the Disney characters.

streets of London begging, poor and hungry. All this reflects on the screen and that's what I like to do—to bring out all those truths."

Other people who have influenced his life are Stevie Wonder, Ray Charles, Chuck Berry, Little Richard, Sammy Davis, Jr., and Sam Cooke. Michael loves classical music and movie musicals.

Michael keeps his career and his fame in proper perspective through his religion. "I believe in God," he says. "We [his family] all do. We like to be straight." He and his mother are Jehovah's Witnesses. Michael goes to Kingdom Hall meetings regularly and does his fieldwork in distributing the *Watch Tower*.

Michael Jackson is a very shy person who prefers to live quietly, keeping his personal life private. Plans are being made for Michael to write his autobiography with editor Jackie Kennedy Onassis, a book that his many fans will welcome. In the meantime Michael has this to say about his future:

"I'm going to be doing a lot of things for people in the future, from the heart. I want to thank everyone through the years, for the sixty-million and everything. And I mean that. Thank you!"

There isn't much more that needs to be said.

Charlie Chaplin in The Gold Rush

Epilogue

IF YOU BELIEVE...

In early 1984 the world was shocked when they heard that Michael had been injured while filming a Pepsi commercial. The scene was the Los Angeles Shrine Auditorium. Suddenly Michael yelled and grabbed his head. His hair was on fire!

Miko Brando, son of Marlon Brando and Michael's bodyguard, was the first to get to him. "I tore out, hugged him, tackled him, and ran my hands through his hair," said Brando, who also suffered minor burns on his hands. Someone grabbed some ice, tore off his shirt, and made a cold ice pack. A few minutes later an ambulance arrived and Michael was rushed to a nearby hospital.

Michael made a rapid recovery, with no permanent damage to his hair or face.

The Jacksons began their "Victory" tour in Kansas City, Missouri, July 6, 1984. Their concert was of the drama, glitter, and glamour that Jackson fans have come to expect. On the eve of the opening night performance, Michael announced that his share of the profits earned on the tour would be given to charity. What will Michael's next move be?

Michael's appearance in a TV commercial for Pepsi-Cola opened the floodgates for statewide Michael Jackson look-alike contests.

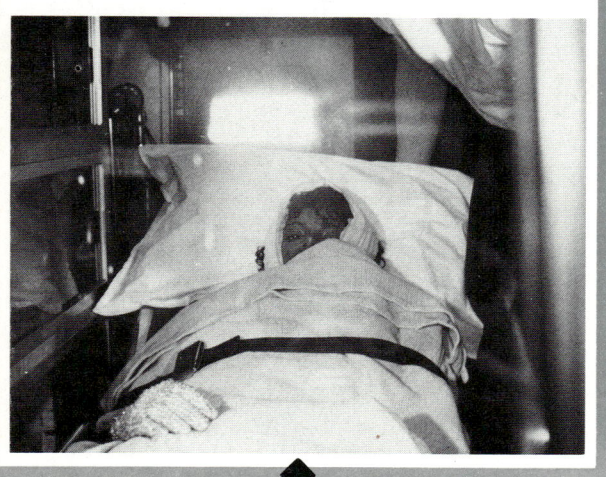

(Above) The Jacksons pose with Don King, boxing promoter and original manager of the Jacksons' 1984 summer tour.

(Left) Michael looks out from an ambulance as he arrives at a hospital. He suffered second degree burns while filming a Pepsi-Cola commercial.

(Right) Jane Fonda, close friend of Michael Jackson, speaks in sign language as she accepts an Oscar for best actress.

Michael is a believer...he believes in the magic that is inside all our hearts. He has also loved J.M. Barrie's book *Peter Pan* ever since he was a young child. Also, it's no secret that Michael has been looking for the right movie since *The Wiz*. It is not surprising then, that Michael's new project is *Peter Pan*. Michael will play the part well; he really believes. "Magic is easy if you put your heart into it," says Michael. "We can fly, you know," he continues. "We just don't know how to think the right thoughts and levitate ourselves off the ground."

Jane Fonda was the first to link Michael with Peter Pan. "I remembered driving him one day," said Jane. "I said 'God, Michael, I wish I could find a movie I could produce for you.' And suddenly I knew. I said, 'I know what you've got to do. It's *Peter Pan*.'

"Tears welled up in his eyes and he said, 'Why did you say that?'

"I said, 'I realize you're Peter Pan.'

"And he started to cry and said, 'You know all over the walls of my room are pictures of Peter Pan. I've read everything that Barrie wrote. I totally identify with Peter Pan, the lost boy of Never-Never Land.'

"Oh, I can see him leading lost children into a world of fantasy and magic...," Jane said.

On May 14, 1984, Michael received an award from President Ronald Reagan for his part in a campaign against drunken driving. Michael's visit to the White House marked the start of national TV and radio ads designed to make young people aware of the dangers involved when they drink and drive. Michael Jackson neither drinks nor smokes. "Beat It" is used to back up the message: "If you don't stop your friend from drinking and driving, you're as good as dead. Drinking and driving can kill a friendship."

Michael Jackson's story is far from over. Millions of fans will eagerly await their chance to see Michael Jackson, Superstar, in person. Millions of others will continue to hear his special sound on videotapes and records and watch his sizzling performances on stage and in the movies. Who knows what other musical revolutions Michael may ignite in the future? The magic of Michael Jackson, the fashion trendsetter and musical genius, has just begun.

From the corner of 23rd and Jackson Street, Gary, Indiana, to the place of honor at the White House, Washington, D.C., a dream comes true—Michael Jackson!

MICHAEL JACKSON TIME LINE

1949: Parents, Joe and Katherine Jackson, marry
1950: Sister Maureen born
1951: Brother Sigmund Esco (Jackie) born
1953: Brother Toriano Adryll (Tito) born
1954: Brother Jermaine born
1956: Sister LaToya born
1957: Brother Marlon David born
1958: Michael Joseph Jackson born August 29 in Gary, Indiana
1961: Brother Steven Randall (Randy) born
1963: Sister Janet born
1964: First Jackson group formed
1965: Michael joins group
1968: Group performs at Apollo Theater in New York
Contract signed with Motown
1969: *Diana Ross Presents the Jackson Five* (Motown)
1970: *ABC* released (Motown)
Grammy for single "ABC" for best pop song of 1970; NAACP "Image Award" for Best Singing Group; *Sixteen* Magazine's "Gold Star" Award as Best Group of Year and for Best Single, "I'll Be There."
1971: TV Special "Goin' Back to Indiana" (ABC)
Album released later in 1971 (gold)
Animated cartoon show, "The Jackson Five," features their singing (ABC)
National Assoc. of Recording Arts and Sciences Award to J-5 for recording Best Pop Song of the Year, "ABC"
January 31: Jackson Five return to Gary, Indiana; 16,000 fans come to hear five of their own perform
1972: Michael records "Ben" (gold)
Michael's solo album *Got to Be There* released by Motown
Jackson Five tour Asia, Australia, Europe, and Africa
1973: "Skywriter" and "Get It Together" released on Motown
1974: "Dancing Machine" released by Motown (gold)
Jackson Five take their act to Las Vegas
1975: June 30: Jackson Five leave Motown label to sign with Epic Records, a large CBS-owned company; Jermaine Jackson remains with Motown
1976: Renamed the Jacksons; record *The Jacksons* released by Epic
Half-hour television show, featuring the Jacksons and sisters, LaToya, Maureen, and Janet

1977: *Goin' Places* released by Epic Records
Michael plays part of Scarecrow in movie version of *The Wiz,* starring Diana Ross, scored by Quincy Jones, and directed by Sidney Lumet

1978: *Destiny* written and produced by the Jacksons
"Ease On Down the Road," soundtrack from the movie *The Wiz*, features Diana Ross and Michael Jackson

1979: *Off the Wall,* Michael's single album (gold) produced by Quincy Jones

1980: Visits the film set of *On Golden Pond*; becomes good friends with Katharine Hepburn and Jane Fonda
Randy seriously injured in car accident
Jermaine's album, *Let's Get Serious,* written and produced by Stevie Wonder, released by Motown (hits Top Ten); *Billboard* magazine names Michael Top Singles Artist and Top Male Vocalist
National Academy of Recording Arts and Sciences votes Michael's "Don't Stop 'Til You Get Enough" as Top Rhythm and Blues Single of the Year

1981: *The Jacksons Live* (2-record set) released by Epic Records

1982: Marlon produces Betty White's album, which has hit single, "She's Older Now"
Janet and LaToya record albums
Jermaine's last album with Motown, *Let Me Tickle Your Fancy,* produced by Jermaine Jackson
"The Girl is Mine," released by Epic, a duet with Michael Jackson and Paul McCartney
Writes the song "Muscle" for Diana Ross album, *Silk Electric,* released by MCA
E.T. The Extra-Terrestrial Storybook released by MCA
Thriller released by Epic; Michael renovates the Encino home to include Disneyland rides and decor

1983: Wins eight Grammy Awards for *Thriller* album

1984: Accidentally burned while filming Pepsi commercial
Confirmed that Michael will play Peter Pan in upcoming film
Honored by President Ronald Reagan for his ad campaigns against drunken driving
Wins MTV awards
Victory album released
Jackson 1984 "Victory" tour begins in Kansas City, Missouri, Jermaine and brothers are reunited.

MICHAEL JACKSON FACT SHEET

Name:	Michael Joseph Jackson
Birthdate:	August 29, 1958
Place of Birth:	Gary, Indiana
Present Address:	Encino, California
Telephone No.:	Unlisted
Religion:	Jehovah's Witness
Zodiac Sign:	Virgo
Color of Hair:	Dark brown
Color of Eyes:	Brown
Height:	5 feet 5 inches
Weight:	Between 120-128 lbs.
Parents:	Joseph and Katherine Jackson
Brothers:	Jackie, Tito, Jermaine, Marlon, Randy
Sisters:	Maureen, LaToya, Janet
Hobbies:	Art, Reading
Best Friend:	Diana Ross
Good Friends:	Jane Fonda, Quincy Jones, Steven Spielberg, Katharine Hepburn
Favorite Books:	*The Greatest Salesman in the World*, by Og Mandino *The Gift of Acabar* by Og Mandino *Johnathan Livingston Seagull* by Richard Bach *The Old Man and the Sea* by Ernest Hemingway
Favorite Foods:	Vegetarian
Recording Studio:	Epic Records, a subsidiary of CBS
Manager:	Joe Jackson
Best Selling Album:	*Thriller*
Best Selling Single:	"Billie Jean"
Girls Dated:	Tatum O'Neal, Stephanie Mills, Brooke Shields
Dislikes:	Crowds, racial bigotry
Likes:	Cartoons, Disneyland rides
Ambition:	To become an actor
Symbol:	The peacock
Pets:	Snake, llama, dogs, cat, birds, sheep
Favorite Actor:	Charlie Chaplin
Favorite Actress:	Katharine Hepburn
Favorite Dancers:	Fred Astaire, Sammy Davis, Jr.
Favorite Singers:	Diana Ross, Stevie Wonder, Barbra Streisand, Jermaine Jackson, Jackie Wilson, Aretha Franklin, Paul McCartney, Sam Cooke, Slim Whitman, Otis Redding

INDEX

"ABC," 12, 26
ABC (album), 26
Academy Awards, 40, 56
American Music Awards, 66
Apollo Theater, Harlem, New York, 19
Astaire, Fred, 77
Bahler, Tom, 66
Baker, Rick, 72
Barrie, J.M., 86, 89
"Beat It," 70, 71, 90
"Beat It" (video), 71, 72, 76, 78
"Ben," 38
Berry, Chuck, 84
Bettis, John, 68
Billboard charts, 52
"Billie Jean," 70, 71, 72, 77
"Billie Jean" (video), 71, 72, 76
"Blame it on the Boogie," 44
Brando, Miko, 86
Brown, James, 16
"bubble-gum sound," 27, 29
Butler, Jerry, 18
"Can You Feel It?", 66
CBS broadcasting network, 42, 71
Charles, Ray, 84
Chicago, Illinois, 19
Chitlin' Circuit, 19, 20
"Climb Every Mountain," 12
Cooke, Sam, 16, 84
"Dancing Machine," 40
Destiny (album), 44, 47
Detroit, Michigan, 22, 24
Diana Ross Presents the Jackson Five (album), 26
"Diff'rent Strokes" (TV show), 35
"Don't Stop 'Til You Get Enough," 66
Dream Girls (Broadway musical), 77
"Ease On Down the Road," 52
Emmy Awards, 77

Encino, California, 36, 47, 62, 80
Epic Records, 42, 44
E.T.: The Extra-Terrestrial (album), 58
Falcons, 8
Fonda, Jane, 56, 57, 63, 89
Gamble, Kenny, 44
Gary, Indiana, 8, 10, 12, 17, 18, 22, 29
Gaye, Marvin, 24
Giraldi, Bob, 63, 71
"Girlfriend," 66
"Girl Is Mine, The," 68
"Goin' Back to Indiana" (TV special), 29
Goin' Places (album), 44
"Good Times" (TV show), 35
Gordy, Berry, Jr., 22, 24-26, 29, 33, 40, 42
Gordy, Hazel, 33
Grammy Awards, 26, 57, 66, 72, 80
Guinness Book of Records, 72
Hatcher, Richard, 22, 29
"Heartbreak Hotel," 67
Hepburn, Katharine, 56, 57
"Hold On, I'm Coming," 16
"Hollywood Palace, The" (TV show), 26
Horne, Lena, 48, 50
Horner, Cynthia, 36, 54
Huff, Leon, 44
"Human Nature," 68
"I'm a Big Boy Now," 18
Indiana, 8, 12, 14, 19
"I Want You Back," 12, 25-26
Jackson, Carol Parker (Marlon's wife), 34
Jackson, DeeDee (Tito's wife), 32
Jackson, Enid Spann (Jackie's wife), 32
Jackson, Hazel Gordy (Jermaine's wife), 33, 34
Jackson, Jackie (Sigmund Esco), 8, 12, 14, 24, 26, 27, 29, 30, 32
Jackson, Janet, 8, 35, 36, 42

Jackson, Jermaine, 8, 12, 14, 20, 26, 27, 32-34, 42
Jackson, Joseph, 8, 10, 11, 14, 17-20, 22, 24, 27, 29, 30, 34, 40, 42
Jackson, Katherine, 8, 10, 11, 14, 17, 19, 20, 27, 29
Jackson, LaToya, 8, 35, 36, 42, 50
Jackson, Marlon David, 8, 14, 26, 27, 30, 32, 34, 47
Jackson, Maureen, 8, 35, 42
Jackson, Randy (Steven Randall), 8, 34, 35, 44
Jackson, Tito (Toriano Adryll), 8, 12, 14, 18, 26, 27, 29, 32, 47
Jackson Five (singing group), 12-42, 74
Jacksons (singing group), 35, 42, 44, 47, 66, 67, 72, 86
Jacksons, The (album), 44
Jackson Street, Gary, Indiana, 8, 10, 11
"Jam Session," 18
Jehovah's Witnesses, 11, 84
Jones, Quincy, 48, 52, 58, 64, 66-68, 70
King, Mabel, 48
"King of Soul Music" (James Brown), 16
Klien, Jill, 76
Knight, Gladys, 18, 22, 24, 26
Lady Sings the Blues (movie), 40
Landis, John, 71, 72
Let's Get Serious (album), 34
Little Richard, 84
Los Angeles, California, 24, 25
Los Angeles Shrine Auditorium, 86
Los Angeles Times newspaper, 67, 83
"Lovely One," 67
Lumet, Sidney, 48, 50
Madison Square Garden, 57
Making of Thriller, The, 71
"Man, The," 70
Martha and the Vandellas, 24

95

MCA (record company), 52
McCartney, Linda, 66
McCartney, Paul, 66, 68, 70
Mercury (record company), 64
MGM Grand, Las Vegas, 40
"Mickey's Monkey," 16
Mills, Stephanie, 58, 78
Minnelli, Liza, 58
Miracles, 16, 24
Mizell, Fonze, 26
Morgan, Rufus, 17
"Motor Town" (Detroit, Michigan), 24
Motown (record company), 18, 22-29, 33, 34, 38, 40, 42
Motown Special (1983), 72, 77
MTV (Music TV), 70
New York City, 19, 51
New York Times newspaper, 70
"Off the Wall," 66
Off the Wall, (album), 66-68, 74
On Golden Pond (movie), 56
Osmond Brothers, 38
Papa Joe's Boys (book), 36
Paper Moon (movie), 78
Parker, Carol, 34
Pepsi commercial, 86
Perren, Freddie, 18, 26
Peter Pan, 86, 89
Peters, Michael, 72, 77, 78

Philadelphia, Pennsylvania, 19
Pitts, Leonard, 36
Porcaro, Steve, 68
Price, Vincent, 68, 71
Pryor, Richard, 48
"P.Y.T." (Pretty Young Thing), 70
Ray, Ola, 71, 72
Reagan, Ronald, 90
Richards, Deke, 26
Richie, Lionel, 76
Right On/Class magazine, 36, 54
Robinson, Smokey, 24, 33
"Rock With You," 66
Rogers, Kenny, 76
Rolling Stone magazine, 63, 78
"Roots" (TV series), 66
Ross, Diana, 22, 24-26, 38, 40, 48, 50, 52, 63, 77
Ross, Ted, 48
Russell, Nipsey, 48
Sam and Dave, 16
"Sanford and Son" (TV show), 32, 66
Save the Children (movie), 51
"Say, Say, Say," 70
"Say, Say, Say" (video), 72
Scholastic Review magazine, 20
"Shake Your Body Down," 35, 44
"She's Out of My Life," 66
Shields, Brooke, 78

"Sin City" (Gary, Indiana), 10
"soul bubble gum," 26
Spann, Enid, 32
Spielberg, Steven, 58, 60
Steeltown (record company), 18
Supremes, 22, 25, 26, 77
Taylor, Bobby, 22
Temperton, Red, 66, 68
Temptations, 16, 20, 24
"Thriller," 68, 71
Thriller (album), 67, 68, 70-72
"Thriller" (video), 71, 72, 74, 78
Time magazine, 17, 18, 80
Tony Awards, 48, 77
Triumph (album), 66
Tug of War (album), 70
Vandellas, Martha and the, 24
Variety magazine, 70
"Walk Right Now," 66
"Wanna Be Startin' Something," 70
"We're Off to See the Wizard," 52
Wiz, The (Broadway play), 48, 58
Wiz, The (movie), 48, 50-53, 66, 89
Wizard of Oz, The (movie), 52, 58
Wonder, Stevie, 19, 24, 34, 84
World Trade Center, 51
Worrell, Denise, 18, 80, 82
"You Can't Win," 52

ABOUT THE AUTHOR

Patricia C. McKissack and her husband, Fredrick, are freelance writers, editors, and teachers of writing. They are the owners and operators of All-Writing Services, located in Clayton, Missouri. Ms. McKissack, an award-winning editor, published author, and experienced educator, has taught writing at several St. Louis colleges and universities, including Lindenwood College, the University of Missouri at St. Louis, and Forest Park Community College.

Since 1975, Ms. McKissack has published numerous magazine articles and stories for juvenile and adult readers. She has also conducted educational and editorial workshops throughout the country for a number of organizations, businesses, and universities.

Patricia McKissack is the mother of three teenage sons. They all live in a large remodeled inner-city home in St. Louis. Aside from writing, which she considers a hobby as well as a career, Ms. McKissack likes to take care of her many plants.